21 Green Fruit And Vegetable Smoothie Snacks: Green Fruit Yogurt Smoothies, Vegan Desserts & Herbal Veggie Bullet Blender Drinks

Juliana Baltimoore

Published by InfinitYou, 2017.

While every precaution has been taken in the preparation of this book, the publisher assumes no responsibility for errors or omissions, or for damages resulting from the use of the information contained herein.

21 GREEN FRUIT AND VEGETABLE SMOOTHIE SNACKS: GREEN FRUIT YOGURT SMOOTHIES, VEGAN DESSERTS & HERBAL VEGGIE BULLET BLENDER DRINKS

First edition. July 11, 2017.

Copyright © 2017 Juliana Baltimoore.

Written by Juliana Baltimoore.

Weight Loss With Smoothies Quiz

A	I	O	A	F	M	W	C	K	C	H	I	A	U	O
V	F	G	H	C	L	K	A	L	E	P	F	E	X	F
V	L	C	W	U	X	F	G	U	D	P	F	M	D	Q
A	Q	V	L	T	R	E	F	P	A	P	A	Y	A	T
E	V	C	D	B	H	S	B	D	E	H	V	W	T	W
T	A	V	O	C	A	D	O	J	P	J	Q	I	J	C
D	S	G	L	U	J	S	P	I	N	A	C	H	R	W
L	L	Y	O	P	A	R	S	L	E	Y	G	H	W	Y
D	P	O	M	E	G	R	A	N	A	T	E	W	T	C
K	I	W	I	H	W	B	L	U	E	B	E	R	R	Y
B	S	R	M	W	C	K	A	H	X	R	B	E	R	B
G	I	N	G	E	R	P	A	U	K	W	R	U	W	S
K	X	R	A	T	R	Y	H	L	H	P	X	Y	M	S
S	D	W	D	B	B	E	F	N	W	Q	H	U	S	S
F	J	L	I	S	H	K	D	K	F	P	G	E	R	G

Ingredients:

1/3 cup of chopped peeled kiwi fruits
1 cup of chopped honeydew melon
1/4 cup of white grape juice
1/2 ripe and sliced banana
1/2 teaspoon of ginger juice
2 teaspoons of fresh lime juice
1/3 cup of unsweeted lemon serbert
1/2 cup of ice

Ingredients:

4 strawberries
1/2 cup of blueberries and/or blackberries
1/2 banana
1 cup of chopped kale
1/2 cup of organic apple juice
1 cup of water
Ice (optional)

1 ripe banana, peeled
1 lg handful spinach, fresh
2 dates, pitted
1 cup blueberries, frozen
1 tbsp. powdered cacao
1 cups water
Ice (optional)

Ingredients:
A few sprays of fresh parsley
1 lemon (no peel) 1 large cucumber (peel if not organic)
4 cups watermelon seeds are ok

Ingredients
1/2 cup of almond milk
1/4 cup of fresh spring water
1/2 cup of frozen blueberries
1/2 banana
1 teaspoon of hemp seeds
1 scoop of vanilla protein powder
1 teaspoon of dried lavender
1/2 tablespoon of maca powder
1 teaspoon of vanilla

Ingredients:

3 Kiwi's (peeled)
1/2 Avocado
1 Banana
4 Cups Spinach
2 Cups Fresh or Frozen Pineapple

Ingredients:

3 Pears
1 Lg Handful of Spinach
1 Cup Fresh or Frozen Raspberries
1 cup water (more if needed)
Ice (optional)

Ingredients:

1 Banana
4 - 6 Dinosaur Kale (remove stems)
1 Pound of Fresh or Frozen Strawberries
1 cup of fresh source water (more if needed)
Ice if you like

Ingredients:

3 Bananas
1 Cup Fresh or Frozen Blueberries
1 Handful Parsley
2 Kale Leaves
1 cup water (more if needed)
Ice (optional)

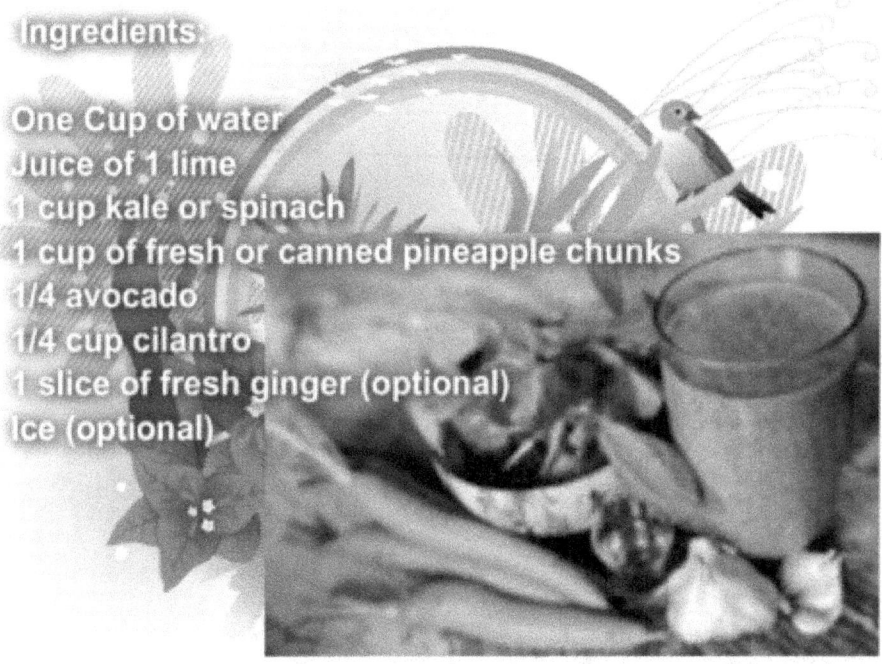

Ingredients:

One Cup of water
Juice of 1 lime
1 cup kale or spinach
1 cup of fresh or canned pineapple chunks
1/4 avocado
1/4 cup cilantro
1 slice of fresh ginger (optional)
Ice (optional)

Ingredients:

1 cup unsweetened almond milk, or coconut milk
1 ripe banana
2 tablespoons of sun butter
1 tablespoon of raw honey
2 tablespoons of unsweetened cocoa powder or raw cacao
Ice (optional)

Ingredients:

1 cup of kale
1 cup of seedless green grapes
1 teaspoon of ground chia seeds
 cup unsweetened almond milk or coconut milk or
2 cups of ice

Ingredients:

1 banana
1 cup of almond milk
1 tablespoon of ground flax seeds
1 large handful of spinach or kale
1 cup of frozen berries
 teaspoon of cinnamon
1 splash of vanilla extract
Ice (optional)

Ingredients:

1 cup of water or unsweetened almond milk, or coconut milk
1 bunch of kale
1 banana
1 orange, peeled
1 teaspoon of vanilla
1 teaspoon of cinnamon
1 dash of cayenne pepper
1-2 tablespoons of ground flax or chia seeds
Ice (optional)

Ingredients:

1 cup of water or unsweetened almond milk or coconut milk
1 green apple, chopped
1/2 avocado
1-2 tablespoons of ground flax or ground chia seeds
5 drops of liquid stevia
a teaspoon of cinnamon
1 dash of nutmeg
1 clove
Ice (optional)

Ingredients:

1 cup of fresh or frozen papaya
1 cup of fresh source water or unsweetened almond milk or coconut milk
1-2 tablespoons ground flax or ground chia seeds
2 cups of chopped kale or spinach
1 splash of vanilla extract
1/8 teaspoon of cinnamon
Ice (optional)

Ingredients:

1 cup of kale
a half cup of parsley leaves (flat leafes)
1 green apple, chopped
1 large banana
1 tablespoon of flax seeds or chia seeds
2 and a half cups of fresh source water
Ice (optional)

Ingredients:

1 cup of frozen berries of your choice
1 cup of spinach
1 cup unsweetened pomegranate juice
Ice (optional)

Ingredients:

1 cup of kale
a half cup of parsley leaves (flat leafes)
1 green apple, chopped
1 large banana
1 tablespoon of flax seeds or chia seeds
2 and a half cups of fresh source water
Ice (optional)

Ingredients:

3 Bananas
1 large Handful of Spinach
5-6 small to Medium Kale Leaves
(instead Kale you can use
Spinach Leaves, too)
1 cup of water
Ice (optional)

Ingredients:

1 cantaloupe
1 cup of Blueberries
4-5 strawberries
a cup of water
Ice (optional)

Introduction

"Next Time, Indiana Jones, it will Take More than Green Smoothies to Save You."—Famous Smoothie Quote

Thank you for purchasing my healthy smoothies recipes that helped me lose 40lbs over two month.

When I lost my weight I started to juice and blend at the same time. What I did was either juice or blend a couple of times a day and I combined it with eating healthy clean foods for 1 meal and a healthy snack or two throughout the day.

The more smoothies you drink during the day and the less processed foods you consume the more weight you are going to lose.

After having gone through this 20 day Smoothie diet (I did it over the time of 2 months), I am feeling so energized and fit.

I had a great experience with this diet and this is why I'd like to share my healthy weight loss smoothie recipes with anyone who would like to lose weight in a quick, delicious and healthy way.

I am also working on a Juicing for weight loss series that you can combine together with these Smoothie recipes for weight loss so that you can enjoy even more variations of these delicious healthy delights that are not only tasty, but they will also make your body lean and clean.

You can check out my Juicing series at the end of the book.

Just one more last tip, these healthy ingredients and nutrients that are inside these smoothies do even become more beneficial to the body and mind if used and consumed in combination with a light yoga workout or any other workout that you prefer.

I always combine it with some Hatha Yoga poses and a daily meditation ritual, but you can use any light workout that you like to do on a daily basis.

Since I have been changing my lifestyle to include healthy smoothies and yoga into my lifestyle, I am fitter than ever before.

Before I had some health issues, stress and sleeping problems, but since I included daily Yoga combined with these healthy smoothies that I am consuming on a regular basis into my lifestyle, I am a new person.

I am so happy that I got started with changing my lifestyle from a common and unhealthy meal plan to one that includes these delicious and healthy smoothies which kind of transformed my life into a balanced, healthy, energized and clean lifestyle!

I am enjoying this lifestyle so much that I decided to motivate and encourage others to get started with these healthy smoothies, too.

Depending on your own goals and preferences, you can either consume them to become a healthier you or you can apply them as a smoothie diet in order to develop a leaner body or to lose some pounds.

Make sure to first consult your doctor or physician to make sure that this diet is a good fit for your own personal situation.

Each smoothie recipe for weight loss includes a list of ingredients that you need to have in order to get started. Each smoothie does not take longer than 5 minute in terms of preparation.

For each Smoothie recipe, simply add all ingredients into a Vitamix or high-speed blender. Add water, if needed, to reach your desired thickness. For all recipes, use organic products, fruits and vegetables when possible.

I include exactly the same recipes that helped me lose 40lbs over two month.

I hope you enjoy the book and I hope that you will get lots of inspiration and stimulation out of the book in order to be able to take advantage and be empowered by the fact that you can lose weight very effectively, but also of the fact that these healthy smoothies are helping you tap into some very powerful health benefits.

Remember, each and every recipe and ingredient has its own benefits for weight loss and health!

All you have to do is identify your goal and take your daily action steps. If you follow my model above, you will have the same success with these delicious and healthy smoothies.

If you are looking to just become healthier, make sure to integrate more and more of these smoothie recipes into your daily meal plan and if you are looking to lose weight, first check with your doctor and then you can follow my smoothie weigh loss model that I explained above.

Everybody has a different goal and you can consume less or more of these smoothies depending on your personal situation, your goal and your lifestyle.

One thing is for sure, if you get yourself into the habit of consuming these smoothies, you will empower and transform your body and mind with the result of a healthier, cleaner, fitter and leaner you! Welcome to the wonderful world of Smoothies!

Weight Loss with Smoothies Story 1: The Blue Hour

"Round up the Usual Fruits and Vegetables." Famous Smoothie Quote

Directions:
For all these Smoothie recipe simply follow these 5 minute directions. Add all the ingredients into your Vitamix or similar high-speed blender. Make sure to add fresh spring water.

Add as much water as you like in order to reach your desired thickness of the smoothie. For all the smoothie recipes, make sure to use organic products, fruits and vegetables if possible.

Mix ¼ cantaloupe, 1 cup Blueberries, 4-5 strawberries, ½ cup of fresh spring water together and add some ice cubes. The ice cubes are totally optional. In the summer adding some more ice is very refreshing.

Enjoy this refreshing and delicious smoothie!

My personal Rules for Weight Loss with these Smoothies:

Blend a couple of times a day and as long as you plan to apply your Smoothie diet

Combine it with eating healthy clean foods for 1 meal and a healthy snack or two throughout the day

Combine your smoothie diet with a light daily workout ritual like Yoga or any other physical activity

The more smoothies you drink during the day and the less processed foods you consume the more weight you are going to lose

Don't push yourself too hard. This is a long term strategy and once you reached your dieting goal, make sure to include these healthy smoothies into your daily meal plan in order to stay fit and keep a lean body

Weight Loss with Smoothies Story 2

"Green Smoothie, I think this is the Beginning of a Beautiful Relationship." Famous Smoothie Quote

Directions:

For all these Smoothie recipe simply follow these 5 minute directions. Add all the ingredients into your Vitamix or similar high-speed blender. Make sure to add fresh spring water.

Add as much water as you like in order to reach your desired thickness of the smoothie. For all the smoothie recipes, make sure to use organic products, fruits and vegetables if possible.

Mix 3 bananas, one large handful of spinach, 5-6 small to medium kale leaves (you can substitute spinach if you like), and one cup of fresh spring water together in your blender. Add ice if needed and to your own liking.

My personal Rules for Weight Loss with these Smoothies:

Blend a couple of times a day and as long as you plan to apply your Smoothie diet

Combine it with eating healthy clean foods for 1 meal and a healthy snack or two throughout the day

Combine your smoothie diet with a light daily workout ritual like Yoga or any other physical activity

The more smoothies you drink during the day and the less processed foods you consume the more weight you are going to lose

Don't push yourself too hard. This is a long term strategy and once you reached your dieting goal, make sure to include these healthy smoothies into your daily meal plan in order to stay fit and keep a lean body

Notes
Weight Loss with Smoothies Story 3

Ingredients:

1 cup of kale
a half cup of parsley leaves (flat leafes)
1 green apple, chopped
1 large banana
1 tablespoon of flax seeds or chia seeds
2 and a half cups of fresh source water
Ice (optional)

"You had me at 'Green Smoothie.'" Famous Smoothie Quote

Directions:

For all these Smoothie recipe simply follow these 5 minute directions. Add all the ingredients into your Vitamix or similar high-speed blender. Make sure to add fresh spring water.

Add as much water as you like in order to reach your desired thickness of the smoothie. For all the smoothie recipes, make sure to use organic products, fruits and vegetables if possible.

Mix 1 cup of kale, 1 green chopped apple, 1 large banana, ½ cup parsley leaves (flat leaf), 1 tablespoon flax meal or chia seeds, 2 ½ cups water and ice (optional).

My personal Rules for Weight Loss with these Smoothies:

Blend a couple of times a day and as long as you plan to apply your Smoothie diet

Combine it with eating healthy clean foods for 1 meal and a healthy snack or two throughout the day

Combine your smoothie diet with a light daily workout ritual like Yoga or any other physical activity

The more smoothies you drink during the day and the less processed foods you consume the more weight you are going to lose

Don't push yourself too hard. This is a long term strategy and once you reached your dieting goal, make sure to include these healthy smoothies into your daily meal plan in order to stay fit and keep a lean body

Notes
Weight Loss with Smoothies Story 4

"May the Smoothie be with you...Always" Famous Smoothie Quote

Directions:

For all these Smoothie recipe simply follow these 5 minute directions. Add all the ingredients into your Vitamix or similar high-speed blender. Make sure to add fresh spring water.

Add as much water as you like in order to reach your desired thickness of the smoothie.

For all the smoothie recipes, make sure to use organic products, fruits and vegetables if possible.

Mix 1 cup frozen berries of your choice, 1 cup of spinach, 1 cup of unsweetened pomegranate juice and some ice. The ice is totally optional.

My personal Rules for Weight Loss with these Smoothies:

Blend a couple of times a day and as long as you plan to apply your Smoothie diet

Combine it with eating healthy clean foods for 1 meal and a healthy snack or two throughout the day

Combine your smoothie diet with a light daily workout ritual like Yoga or any other physical activity

The more smoothies you drink during the day and the less processed foods you consume the more weight you are going to lose

Don't push yourself too hard. This is a long term strategy and once you reached your dieting goal, make sure to include these healthy smoothies into your daily meal plan in order to stay fit and lean. bo

Weight Loss with Smoothies Story 5

Ingredients:
1 cup of kale
a half cup of parsley leaves (flat leafes)
1 green apple, chopped
1 large banana
1 tablespoon of flax seeds or chia seeds
2 and a half cups of fresh source water
Ice (optional)

"All Great Things are Simple, and Many can be Expressed in Single Words: Freedom, Justice, Honor, Duty, Mercy, Hope, Smoothies." Famous Smoothie Quote

Directions:

For all these Smoothie recipe simply follow these 5 minute directions. Add all the ingredients into your Vitamix or similar high-speed blender. Make sure to add fresh spring water.

Add as much water as you like in order to reach your desired thickness of the smoothie. For all the smoothie recipes, make sure to use organic products, fruits and vegetables if possible.

Mix 1 cup of unsweetened almond milk, hemp milk, or coconut milk, 1 handful of kale or spinach, 1 cup of blueberries, ¼ teaspoon of cinnamon, 1 teaspoon of spirulina (this is totally optional), 1 splash of organic vanilla extract and some ice. The ice is totally optional.

My personal Rules for Weight Loss with these Smoothies:

Blend a couple of times a day and as long as you plan to apply your Smoothie diet

Combine it with eating healthy clean foods for 1 meal and a healthy snack or two throughout the day

Combine your smoothie diet with a light daily workout ritual like Yoga or any other physical activity

The more smoothies you drink during the day and the less processed foods you consume the more weight you are going to lose

Don't push yourself too hard. This is a long term strategy and once you reached your dieting goal, make sure to include these healthy smoothies into your daily meal plan in order to stay fit and keep a lean body

Weight Loss with Smoothies Story 6

Ingredients:

1 cup of fresh or frozen papaya
1 cup of fresh source water or unsweetened almond milk or coconut milk
1-2 tablespoons ground flax or ground chia seeds
2 cups of chopped kale or spinach
1 splash of vanilla extract
1/8 teaspoon of cinnamon
Ice (optional)

"Not that I loved Ceasar Salads Less, but that I loved Green Smoothies More" Famous Smoothie Quote

Directions:
   For all these Smoothie recipe simply follow these 5 minute directions. Add all the ingredients into your Vitamix or similar high-speed blender. Make sure to add fresh spring water.

Add as much water as you like in order to reach your desired thickness of the smoothie. For all the smoothie recipes, make sure to use organic products, fruits and vegetables if possible.

Mix ½ cup of fresh or frozen papaya fruit, 1 cup of fresh spring water or unsweetened almond milk, hemp milk, or coconut milk, 1-2 tablespoon of ground flax or ground chia seeds, 2 cups of chopped kale or spinach, 1/8 teaspoon of cinnamon and 1 splash of organic vanilla extract and some ice cubes (this is totally optional).

My personal Rules for Weight Loss with these Smoothies:

Blend a couple of times a day and as long as you plan to apply your Smoothie diet

Combine it with eating healthy clean foods for 1 meal and a healthy snack or two throughout the day

Combine your smoothie diet with a light daily workout ritual like Yoga or any other physical activity

The more smoothies you drink during the day and the less

processed foods you consume the more weight you are going to lose

Don't push yourself too hard. This is a long term strategy and once you reached your dieting goal, make sure to include these healthy smoothies into your daily meal plan in order to stay fit and keep a lean body.

Weight Loss with Smoothies Story 7

Ingredients:

1 cup of water or unsweetened almond milk or coconut milk
1 green apple, chopped
1/2 avocado
1-2 tablespoons of ground flax or ground chia seeds
5 drops of liquid stevia
a teaspoon of cinnamon
1 dash of nutmeg
1 clove
Ice (optional)

"A Green Smoothie is Worth a Thousand Donuts"
Famous Smoothie Quote

Directions:

For all these Smoothie recipe simply follow these 5 minute directions. Add all the ingredients into your Vitamix or similar high-speed blender. Make sure to add fresh spring water. Add as much water as you like in order to reach your desired thickness of the smoothie. For all the smoothie recipes, make sure to use organic products, fruits and vegetables if possible.

Mix 1 cup of fresh spring water or unsweetened almond milk, hemp milk, rice milk, or coconut milk, 1 fresh and chopped green apple, ½ avocado, 1-2 tablespoons of ground flax or ground chia seeds, 5 drops of liquid stevia, ½ teaspoon of cinnamon, 1 dash of nutmeg, 1 clove, and some ice cubes.

The ice cubes are totally optional.

My personal Rules for Weight Loss with these Smoothies:

Blend a couple of times a day and as long as you plan to apply your Smoothie diet

Combine it with eating healthy clean foods for 1 meal and a healthy snack or two throughout the day

Combine your smoothie diet with a light daily workout ritual like Yoga or any other physical activity

The more smoothies you drink during the day and the less processed foods you consume the more weight you are going to lose

Don't push yourself too hard. This is a long term strategy and once you reached your dieting goal, make sure to include these healthy smoothies into your daily meal plan in order to stay fit and keep a lean body.

Weight Loss with Smoothies Story 8

"There are More Good Things in Green Smoothies, Horatio, Than are Dreamt of in your Meat and Potatoes Philosophy." Famous Smoothie Quote

Directions:

For all these Smoothie recipe simply follow these 5 minute directions. Add all the ingredients into your Vitamix or similar high-speed blender. Make sure to add fresh spring water. Add as much water as you like in order to reach your desired thickness of the smoothie. For all the smoothie recipes, make sure to use organic products, fruits and vegetables if possible.

Mix 1 cup of fresh spring water or unsweetened almond milk, coconut milk, hemp milk, or rice milk, ½ bunch of kale, 1 ripe banana, ½ peeled orange, 1 teaspoon of organic vanilla, 1 teaspoon of cinnamon, 1 dash of cayenne pepper, 1-2 tablespoons of ground flax or chia seeds and ice. The ice is totally optional.

My personal Rules for Weight Loss with these Smoothies:

Blend a couple of times a day and as long as you plan to apply your Smoothie diet

Combine it with eating healthy clean foods for 1 meal and a healthy snack or two throughout the day

Combine your smoothie diet with a light daily workout ritual like Yoga or any other physical activity

The more smoothies you drink during the day and the less processed foods you consume the more weight you are going to lose

Don't push yourself too hard.

This is a long term strategy and once you reached your dieting goal, make sure to include these healthy smoothies into your daily meal plan in order to stay fit and keep a lean body

Weight Loss with Smoothies Story 9

"What's in a Name? That which we call a Green Smoothie By any Other Name would Taste as Sweet." Famous Smoothie Quote

Directions:

For all these Smoothie recipe simply follow these 5 minute directions. Add all the ingredients into your Vitamix or similar high-speed blender. Make sure to add fresh spring water. Add as much water as you like in order to reach your desired thickness of the smoothie. For all the smoothie recipes, make sure to use organic products, fruits and vegetables if possible.

Mix 1 ripe banana, 1 cup of almond milk, 1 tablespoon of ground flax seed, 1 large handful spinach or kale, 1 cup of frozen berries, ¼ teaspoon of cinnamon, 1 splash of organic vanilla extract and some ice (completely optional).

My personal Rules for Weight Loss with these Smoothies:

Blend a couple of times a day and as long as you plan to apply your Smoothie diet

Combine it with eating healthy clean foods for 1 meal and a healthy snack or two throughout the day

Combine your smoothie diet with a light daily workout ritual like Yoga or any other physical activity

The more smoothies you drink during the day and the less processed foods you consume the more weight you are going to lose

Don't push yourself too hard. This is a long term strategy and once you reached your dieting goal, make sure to include these healthy smoothies into your daily meal plan in order to stay fit

and keep a lean body

Weight Loss with Smoothies Story 10

Ingredients:

1 cup of kale
1 cup of seedless green grapes
1 teaspoon of ground chia seeds
 cup unsweetened almond milk or coconut milk or
2 cups of ice

The first day I was like, 'Oh, dear God,' because the green juice tastes like what you smell when the lawn has been mowed ... Now I call it liquid gold... Minneapolis Star Tribune

Directions:
For all these Smoothie recipe simply follow these 5 minute directions. Add all the ingredients into your Vitamix or similar high-speed blender. Make sure to add fresh spring water. Add as much water as you like in order to reach your desired thickness of the smoothie. For all the smoothie recipes, make sure to use organic products, fruits and vegetables if possible.

Mix 1 cup of kale, 1 cup of seedless green grapes, 1 teaspoon of ground chia seeds, ½ cup of unsweetened almond milk, coconut milk or hemp milk and 2 cups of ice.

The ice is totally optional.

My personal Rules for Weight Loss with these Smoothies:

Blend a couple of times a day and as long as you plan to apply your Smoothie diet

Combine it with eating healthy clean foods for 1 meal and a healthy snack or two throughout the day

Combine your smoothie diet with a light daily workout ritual like Yoga or any other physical activity

The more smoothies you drink during the day and the less processed foods you consume the more weight you are going to lose

Don't push yourself too hard. This is a long term strategy and once you reached your dieting goal, make sure to include these healthy smoothies into your daily meal plan in order to stay fit and keep a lean body

Weight Loss with Smoothies Story 11

Ingredients:

1 cup unsweetened almond milk, or coconut milk
1 ripe banana
2 tablespoons of sun butter
1 tablespoon of raw honey
2 tablespoons of unsweetened cocoa powder or raw cacao
Ice (optional)

I knew I had to improve ... I tried high carb, low carb, high protein, low protein, all sorts of different diets. Then I tried plant-based. It started with me just taking a daily blender drink of fats, plants, proteins... Bangor Daily New

Directions:
   For all these Smoothie recipe simply follow these 5 minute directions. Add all the ingredients into your Vitamix or similar high-speed blender. Make sure to add fresh spring water. Add as much water as you like in order to reach your

desired thickness of the smoothie. For all the smoothie recipes, make sure to use organic products, fruits and vegetables if possible.

Mix 1 cup of unsweetened almond milk, coconut milk, hemp milk, or rice milk, 1 ripe banana, 2 tablespoons of sun butter, 1 tablespoon of raw honey or stevia, 2 tablespoons of unsweetened and organic cocoa powder. You can also use raw cacao.

Add some ice. The ice is totally optional.

My personal Rules for Weight Loss with these Smoothies:

Blend a couple of times a day and as long as you plan to apply your Smoothie diet

Combine it with eating healthy clean foods for 1 meal and a healthy snack or two throughout the day

Combine your smoothie diet with a light daily workout ritual like Yoga or any other physical activity

The more smoothies you drink during the day and the less processed foods you consume the more weight you are going to lose

Don't push yourself too hard. This is a long term strategy and once you reached your dieting goal, make sure to include these healthy smoothies into your daily meal plan in order to stay fit and keep a lean body

Weight Loss with Smoothies Story 12

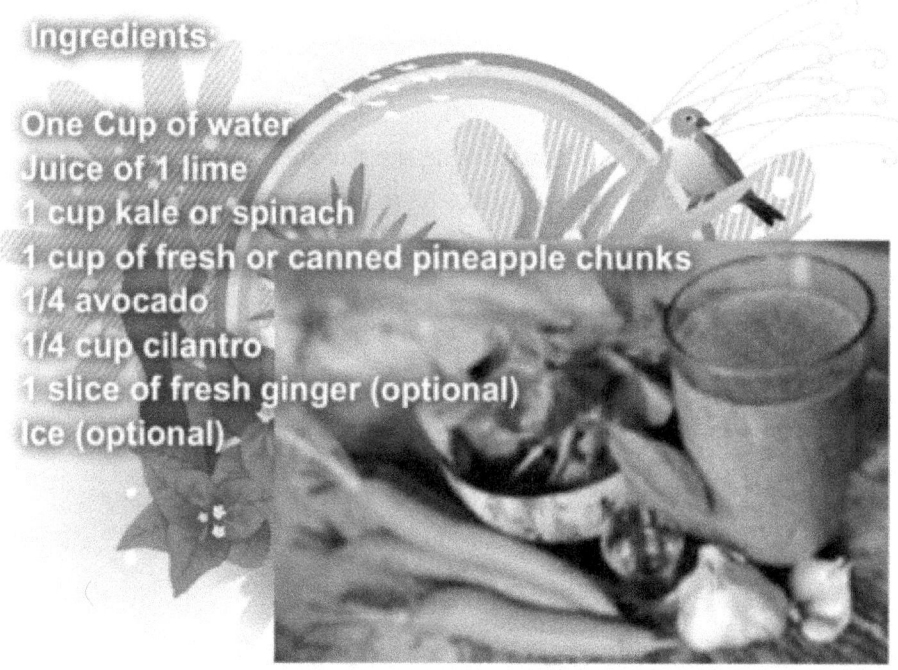

Ingredients
One Cup of water
Juice of 1 lime
1 cup kale or spinach
1 cup of fresh or canned pineapple chunks
1/4 avocado
1/4 cup cilantro
1 slice of fresh ginger (optional)
Ice (optional)

"All Right, Mr. DeMille, I'm Ready for my Green Smoothie." Famous Smoothie Quote

Directions:

For all these Smoothie recipe simply follow these 5 minute directions. Add all the ingredients into your Vitamix or similar high-speed blender. Make sure to add fresh spring water.

Add as much water as you like in order to reach your desired thickness of the smoothie. For all the smoothie recipes, make sure to use organic products, fruits and vegetables if possible.

Mix ¾ cup water, juice of 1 fresh lime, 1 cup of fresh kale or spinach, 1 cup of fresh pineapple chunks, ¼ avocado, ¼ cup of cilantro, 1 slice of ginger and some ice which is optional.

My personal Rules for weight loss with these Smoothies:

Blend a couple of times a day and as long as you plan to apply your Smoothie diet

Combine it with eating healthy clean foods for 1 meal and a healthy snack or two throughout the day

Combine your smoothie diet with a light daily workout ritual like Yoga or any other physical activity

The more smoothies you drink during the day and the less processed foods you consume the more weight you are going to lose

Don't push yourself too hard. This is a long term strategy and once you reached your dieting goal, make sure to include these healthy smoothies into your daily meal plan in order to stay fit and keep a lean body

Notes

Notes

Weight Loss with Smoothies Story 13

"Knowing is not enough; we must apply. Willing is not enough; we must do." Johann von Goethe

Directions:
For all these Smoothie recipe simply follow these 5 minute directions. Add all the ingredients into your Vitamix or similar high-speed blender. Make sure to add fresh spring water.

Add as much water as you like in order to reach your desired thickness of the smoothie.

For all the smoothie recipes, make sure to use organic products, fruits and vegetables if possible.

Mix 3 bananas, 1 cup of fresh or frozen blueberries, 1 handful of fresh parsley, 2 fresh kale leaves, 1 cup of fresh spring water (more if needed) and some ice (optional).

My personal Rules for Weight Loss with these Smoothies:

Blend a couple of times a day and as long as you plan to apply your Smoothie diet

Combine it with eating healthy clean foods for 1 meal and a healthy snack or two throughout the day

Combine your smoothie diet with a light daily workout ritual like Yoga or any other physical activity

The more smoothies you drink during the day and the less processed foods you consume the more weight you are going to lose

Don't push yourself too hard. This is a long term strategy and once you reached your dieting goal, make sure to include these healthy smoothies into your daily meal plan in order to stay fit and keep a lean body

Notes
Weight Loss with Smoothies Story 14

Ingredients:

1 Banana
4 - 6 Dinosaur Kale (remove stems)
1 Pound of Fresh or Frozen Strawberries
1 cup of fresh source water (more if needed)
Ice if you like

"Health is a state of complete physical, mental and social well-being, and not merely the absence of disease or infirmity." World Health Organization

Directions:
For all these Smoothie recipe simply follow these 5 minute directions. Add all the ingredients into your Vitamix or similar high-speed blender. Make sure to add fresh spring water. Add as much water as you like in order to reach your

desired thickness of the smoothie. For all the smoothie recipes, make sure to use organic products, fruits and vegetables if possible.

Mix 1 ripe and peeled banana, 4 - 6 dinosaur kale (remove it from stems), 1 pound of fresh or frozen strawberries, 1 cup of fresh spring water (more if needed) and ice if you like.

The ice is totally optional.

My personal Rules for Weight Loss with these Smoothies:

Blend a couple of times a day and as long as you plan to apply your Smoothie diet

Combine it with eating healthy clean foods for 1 meal and a healthy snack or two throughout the day

Combine your smoothie diet with a light daily workout ritual like Yoga or any other physical activity

The more smoothies you drink during the day and the less processed foods you consume the more weight you are going to lose

Don't push yourself too hard. This is a long term strategy and once you reached your dieting goal, make sure to include these healthy smoothies into your daily meal plan in order to stay fit and keep a lean body

Weight Loss with Smoothies Story 15

"Our health always seems much more valuable after we lose it." Unknown

21 GREEN FRUIT AND VEGETABLE SMOOTHIE SNACKS: GREEN FRUIT YOGURT SMOOTHIES, VEGAN DESSERTS & HERBAL VEGGIE BULLET BLENDER DRINKS

Directions:

For all these Smoothie recipe simply follow these 5 minute directions. Add all the ingredients into your Vitamix or similar high-speed blender. Make sure to add fresh spring water.

Add as much water as you like in order to reach your desired thickness of the smoothie. For all the smoothie recipes, make sure to use organic products, fruits and vegetables if possible.

Mix 3 pears, 1 large handful of fresh spinach, 1 cup of fresh or frozen raspberries, 1 cup of fresh spring water (use more water if needed) and some ice (optional).

My personal Rules for weight loss with these Smoothies:

Blend a couple of times a day and as long as you plan to apply your Smoothie diet

Combine it with eating healthy clean foods for 1 meal and a healthy snack or two throughout the day

Combine your smoothie diet with a light daily workout ritual like Yoga or any other physical activity

The more smoothies you drink during the day and the less processed foods you consume the more weight you are going to lose

Don't push yourself too hard. This is a long term strategy and once you reached your dieting goal, make sure to include these healthy smoothies into your daily meal plan in order to stay fit and keep a lean body

Weight Loss with Smoothies Story 16

Ingredients:

3 Kiwi's (peeled)
1/2 Avocado
1 Banana
4 Cups Spinach
2 Cups Fresh or Frozen Pineapple

"A man's health can be judged by which he takes two at a time - pills or stairs." Joan Welsh

Directions:

For all these Smoothie recipe simply follow these 5 minute directions. Add all the ingredients into your Vitamix or similar high-speed blender. Make sure to add fresh spring water.

Add as much water as you like in order to reach your desired thickness of the smoothie. For all the smoothie recipes, make sure to use organic products, fruits and vegetables if possible.

Mix 3 peeled kiwis, 1/2 avocado, 1 banana, 4 cups of fresh spinach, 2 cups of fresh or frozen pineapple and some ice.

The ice is totally optional.

My personal Rules for Weight Loss with these Smoothies:

Blend a couple of times a day and as long as you plan to apply your Smoothie diet

Combine it with eating healthy clean foods for 1 meal and a healthy snack or two throughout the day

Combine your smoothie diet with a light daily workout ritual like Yoga or any other physical activity

The more smoothies you drink during the day and the less processed foods you consume the more weight you are going to lose

Don't push yourself too hard. This is a long-term strategy and once you reached your dieting goal, make sure to include these healthy smoothies into your daily meal plan in order to stay fit and keep a lean body

Weight Loss with Smoothies Story 17

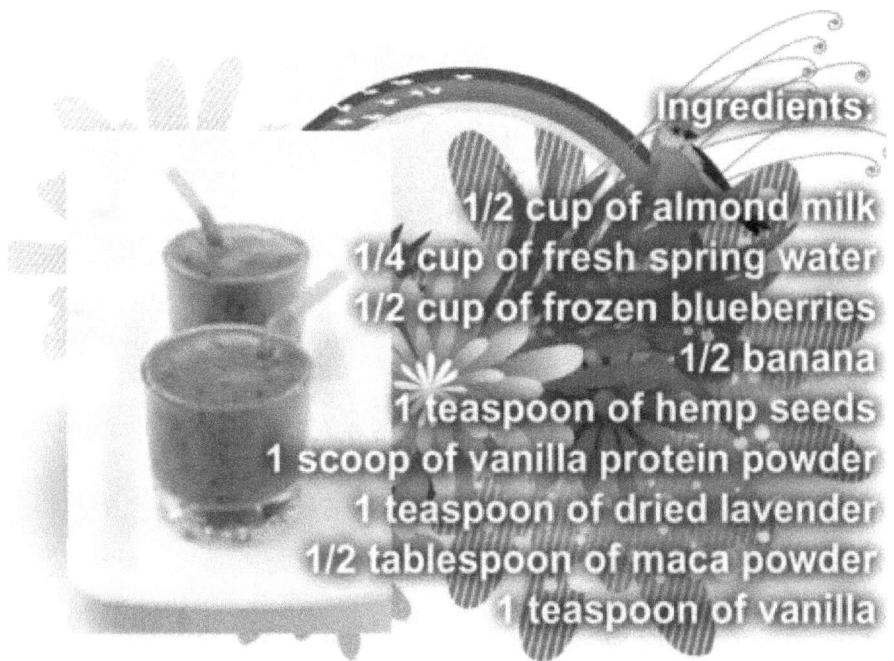

Ingredients:
1/2 cup of almond milk
1/4 cup of fresh spring water
1/2 cup of frozen blueberries
1/2 banana
1 teaspoon of hemp seeds
1 scoop of vanilla protein powder
1 teaspoon of dried lavender
1/2 tablespoon of maca powder
1 teaspoon of vanilla

"Choice, not chance, determines destiny." E.C. McKenzie

Directions:
For all these Smoothie recipe simply follow these 5 minute directions. Add all the ingredients into your Vitamix or similar high-speed blender. Make sure to add fresh spring water. Add as much water as you like in order to reach your desired thickness of the smoothie.

For all the smoothie recipes, make sure to use organic products, fruits and vegetables if possible.

This smoothie has the antioxidant power of blueberries plus the energy boosting power of the maca powder. Maca is a root that Incan warriors used for strength and endurance.

Mix ½ cup almond milk, ¼ cup water, ½ cup frozen blueberries, ½ banana, 1 teaspoon of hemp seeds, 1 scoop of vanilla protein powder, 1 teaspoon of dried lavender, ½ tablespoon of maca powder and one 1 teaspoon of organic vanilla.

My personal Rules for Weight Loss with these Smoothies:

Blend a couple of times a day and as long as you plan to apply your Smoothie diet

Combine it with eating healthy clean foods for 1 meal and a healthy snack or two throughout the day

Combine your smoothie diet with a light daily workout ritual like Yoga or any other physical activity

The more smoothies you drink during the day and the less processed foods you consume the more weight you are going to lose

Don't push yourself too hard. This is a long term strategy and once you reached your dieting goal, make sure to include these healthy smoothies into your daily meal plan in order to stay fit and keep a lean body

Weight Loss with Smoothies Story 18

Ingredients:
A few sprays of fresh parsley
1 lemon (no peel) 1 large cucumber (peel if not organic)
4 cups watermelon seeds are ok

"This one step - choosing a goal and sticking to it - changes everything." Scott Reed

Directions:

For all these Smoothie recipe simply follow these 5 minute
directions. Add all the ingredients into your Vitamix or similar high-speed blender. Make sure to add fresh spring water.

Add as much water as you like in order to reach your desired thickness of the smoothie. For all the smoothie recipes, make sure to use organic products, fruits and vegetables if possible.

Mix a few sprays of fresh parsley, 1 lemon (no lemon peel) 1 large cucumber (peel the cucumber if it is not organic), 4 cups of watermelon seeds.

Add some additional ice to your liking.

My personal Rules for Weight Loss with these Smoothies:

Blend a couple of times a day and as long as you plan to apply your Smoothie diet

Combine it with eating healthy clean foods for 1 meal and a healthy snack or two throughout the day

Combine your smoothie diet with a light daily workout ritual like Yoga or any other physical activity

The more smoothies you drink during the day and the less processed foods you consume the more weight you are going to lose

Don't push yourself too hard. This is a long term strategy and once you reached your dieting goal, make sure to include these healthy smoothies into your daily meal plan in order to stay fit and keep a lean body

Notes

Weight Loss with Smoothies Story 19

1 ripe banana, peeled
1 lg handful spinach, fresh
2 dates, pitted
1 cup blueberries, frozen
1 tbsp. powdered cacao
1 cups water
Ice (optional)

"Movement is a medicine for creating change in a person's physical, emotional, and mental states." Carol Welch

Directions:

For all these Smoothie recipe simply follow these 5 minute directions. Add all the ingredients into your Vitamix or similar high-speed blender. Make sure to add fresh spring water. Add as much water as you like in order to reach your desired thickness of the smoothie. For all the smoothie recipes, make sure to use organic products, fruits and vegetables if possible.

21 GREEN FRUIT AND VEGETABLE SMOOTHIE SNACKS: GREEN FRUIT YOGURT SMOOTHIES, VEGAN DESSERTS & HERBAL VEGGIE BULLET BLENDER DRINKS

Mix 1 ripe and peeled banana, 1 large handful of fresh spinach, 2 pitted dates, 1 cup of frozen blueberries, 1 tablespoon of organic powdered cacao, 1 ½ cups of fresh spring water and some ice cubes that are optional.

My personal Rules for Weight Loss with these Smoothies:

Blend a couple of times a day and as long as you plan to apply your Smoothie diet

Combine it with eating healthy clean foods for 1 meal and a healthy snack or two throughout the day

Combine your smoothie diet with a light daily workout ritual like Yoga or any other physical activity

The more smoothies you drink during the day and the less processed foods you consume the more weight you are going to lose

Don't push yourself too hard. This is a long term strategy and once you reached your dieting goal, make sure to include these healthy smoothies into your daily meal plan in order to stay fit and keep a lean body

Weight Loss with Smoothies Story 20

Ingredients:
4 strawberries
1/2 cup of blueberries and/or blackberries
1/2 banana
1 cup of chopped kale
1/2 cup of organic apple juice
1 cup of water
Ice (optional)

"We Are such Stuff As Green Smoothies are Made of..." Famous Smoothie Quote

Directions:

For all these Smoothie recipe simply follow these 5 minute directions. Add all the ingredients into your Vitamix or similar high-speed blender. Make sure to add fresh spring water. Add as much water as you like in order to reach your desired thickness of the smoothie.

For all the smoothie recipes, make sure to use organic products, fruits and vegetables if possible.

Mix 4 strawberries, 1/2 cup of blueberries and/or blackberries, 1/2 banana, 1 cup of chopped kale, 1/2 cup of organic apple juice, 1 cup of water, and some ice (totally optional).

My personal Rules for Weight Loss with these Smoothies:

Blend a couple of times a day and as long as you plan to apply your Smoothie diet

Combine it with eating healthy clean foods for 1 meal and a healthy snack or two throughout the day

Combine your smoothie diet with a light daily workout ritual like Yoga or any other physical activity

The more smoothies you drink during the day and the less processed foods you consume the more weight you are going to lose

Don't push yourself too hard. This is a long term strategy and once you reached your dieting goal, make sure to include these healthy smoothies into your daily meal plan in order to stay fit and keep a lean body

Weight Loss with Smoothies Story 21

Ingredients:

1/3 cup of chopped peeled kiwi fruits
1 cup of chopped honeydew melon
1/4 cup of white grape juice
1/2 ripe and sliced banana
1/2 teaspoon of ginger juice
2 teaspoons of fresh lime juice
1/3 cup of unsweeted lemon serbert
1/2 cup of ice

"It's not that some people have willpower and some don't. It's that some people are ready to change and others are not." James Gordon

Directions:

For all these Smoothie recipe simply follow these 5 minute directions. Add all the ingredients into your Vitamix or similar high-speed blender. Make sure to add fresh spring water. Add as much water as you like in order to reach your

desired thickness of the smoothie. For all the smoothie recipes, make sure to use organic products, fruits and vegetables if possible.

Mix 1/3 cup of chopped peeled kiwi fruits, 1 cup of chopped honeydew melon, 1/4 cup of white grape juice, 1/2 ripe and sliced banana, 1/2 teaspoon of ginger juice, 2 teaspoons of fresh lime juice, 1/3 cup of unsweetened lemon sherbert and 1/2 cup of ice together.

Pulse the mixture three times with your Vitamix or blender. Chop the fruits and then blend the mixture until it has a nice and smooth texture. Serve the Honeydew Ginger Blend immediately and enjoy!

Bottled ginger juice is available in most health or health food stores or in some gourmet markets. You can also make the ginger juice yourself by squeezing the fresh and chopped ginger through a piece of cheese cloth or by using a press (best is a garlic press).

My personal Rules for Weight Loss with these Smoothies

Blend a couple of times a day and as long as you plan to apply your Smoothie diet

Combine it with eating healthy clean foods for 1 meal and a healthy snack or two throughout the day

Combine your smoothie diet with a light daily workout ritual like Yoga or any other physical activity

The more smoothies you drink during the day and the less processed foods you consume the more weight you are going to lose

Don't push yourself too hard. This is a long term strategy and once you reached your dieting goal, make sure to include these healthy smoothies into your daily meal plan in order to stay fit and keep a lean body.

Pro Tips For Smoothies

These are some pro tips you can apply to these healthy smoothies to make your weight management even more effective:

Be sure to pour in liquids first (it's less complicated on the whisker).

Start from the lowest speed and work up to higher speeds once the blend smoothis out. Add ice last, and use as much or as little as you'd like.

I suggest 3 cubes for each smoothie, but it is brilliantly OK to add more and make it a little slushier to attain a creamier texture. Some of my smoothies use cow's milk, or dairy free subs like almond, coconut, soy, hemp, and rice milk.

Pick your favorite, or make a mix of your own.

If you have leftover smoothie hanging in the whisker, divvy it up into an ice cube tray for simple mixing next time.

Top smoothies with fresh fruit, seeds, sliced nuts, or shredded coconut for a texture change.

Try making an oatmeal, flax seed, orange, and pineapple smoothie.

Freeze fruit for a heavier consistency.

Chop it up for simpler mixing.

Maximise Your Smoothies For Weight Loss

"There are two primary choices in life: to accept conditions as they exist, or accept the responsibility for changing them." ~Dr. Denis Waitley

Maximize Your Smoothies For Weight Management

The most significant advantage of using smoothies for weightloss is they cause you to feel full. When you cut down on calories, it's only natural you are going to feel hungry. When you're feeling hungry all of the time, it is difficult not to focus upon food that will lead to nibbling. For many folks, nibbling leads to over-indulging which then leads to sensations of inadequacy which in turn leads to an unsuccessful diet.

Luckily, smoothies can help break this cycle. A thick smoothie will lead you to feel full. If you do not feel hungry, you will not think about food all of the time and your diet will be more successful.

When you also consider that some ingredients can also help in promoting weight management, smoothies are the ideal break when attempting to shed weight.

I am constantly trying new weight loss smoothie recipes and to individualize my diet Smoothies. These are my proposals for making changes and for making these healthy Smoothies even more effective for a diet. These are very useful tips if your goal is to lose weight with these Smoothies because you will learn how to maximize these smoothies for weight loss.

Use nonfat or low fat yogurt This is blazingly obvious, but it is critical to say. If the smoothie recipe requires ice cream, you can substitute frozen fat free yogurt. Again, I adore vanilla so I generally use vanilla-flavored nonfat yogurt. You can also use nonfat and unsweetened sherbert like the Italian type of lemon sherbert. Make sure to get the unsweetened version or make it yourself without sugar.

Add nuts and seeds. Almonds are a great addition if your objective is to form smoothies for weight management.

Use fortified soya milk rather than dairy milk. Soya milk only has about seven grams of sugar per cup while cow milk has about twelve grams. A cup of soya milk has about eighty calories. Dairy milk and soya milk have about an identical quantity of protein and carbs.

Nonetheless fortified soya milk have bigger amounts of omega fats (which are healthy for your heart), micronutrients, and isoflavones.

Research has shown that soy beans can scale back your cholesterol. It raises the level of high density lipoproteins (HDL) in your blood stream and noticeably decreases the quantity of low density lipoproteins (LDL) and triglycerides.

It's possible to get vanilla flavored soya milk which makes your smoothies for weight management far more succulent and deliciously tasty!

Many of us back away from them because they're heavy in calories, but they're essentially extraordinarily advantageous when referring to shedding weight.

Almonds are fat-heavy which helps cause you to feel full. The fat content is "healthy fat". The Omega-3 trans acids help in reducing your body's fat and help increase the quantity of lean muscle tissue in your body.

Entire flax seeds add a pleasant nutty flavour and a crunchy texture plus they add additional micronutrients and fiber. You may try experimenting with other nuts and seeds to find your own tops.

Fiber helps super-charge your smoothies for weight loss. Diet fiber causes you to feel full quicker. It also makes it take more time to eat and digest, which helps combat over indulging. This is why you should add more fiber to your smoothies and especially if you are using them for the purpose of weight loss.

Some fruits have more fiber than others.

Raspberries, for instance, taste superb and have about eight grams of diet fiber per cup.

Using the entire fruit if possible will also add to your smoothie's fiber content.

With some fruit, like apples, the skin is more fit than the remainder of the fruit. In most fruits, the seeds, stem, core, and pith each contain valuable nutriments. And they add additional fiber.

Do not be concerned that they'll make your smoothie taste bad. If you happen to have a proper blener like a Vitamix or any other alternative, they'll get mixed so well into your diet smoothie that you won't even know they're there.

Use Splenda rather than sugar. Some of the fruits utilized in weight reduction smoothies have a sour taste. Sour fruits have a tendency to have plenty of polyphenolic acids which are good anti oxidising compounds. If you do not like the taste, don't cut them out of the smoothie recipe.

As an alternative add a little bit of Splenda to sweeten it up.

I feel I must mention that there are several folk who believe Splenda is not good for you. There are numerous websites detailing possible risks or complications of consuming Splenda. To be truthful, I'm on the fence about this. I do use Splenda now and then but I also make efforts not to use it if I potentially can.

At the day's close, though, I'm not a doctor nor a diet consultant. Do the analysis and do what you're feeling is best for you.

Use Bananas and pineapple juice. Ripe bananas and pineapple juice are the most typical ingredients in my weight management smoothies.

They're inexpensive, freely available, add additional nutrient elements, and go with nearly any smoothie recipe (a combination of bananas and/or pineapple with vanilla equals a fantastic taste).

In reality if you do not wish to add Splenda, you need to use pineapple juice to naturally sweeten up any smoothie recipe.

Pineapple juice is a useful source of vitamin C and potassium. It's also rick in Thiamine, a soluble vitamin in the B group of vitamins.

Thiamine helps convert carbs into energy and will also help maintain a good nerve system and clearness.

If you can use full fruits rather than bottled or canned fruit juices for your weight management smoothies. Most fruit juices are so highly processed that there's little left in them except colour and taste. Using the entire fruit rather than the juice will ensure you get the maximum nutrient elements and the highest benefits.

Add more "super fruits" to your weight loss smoothies.

Supposed "super fruits" are loaded in prebiotic fiber, vitamin C (the universal anti-oxidant), carotenoids, and polyphenols. I am not a nutrition expert, so I'm not going to go into their health benefits here. Just remember that some fruits are much better than others and use that information when you're making substitutions to a smoothie for weight management.

Super fruits include red guava, oranges, strawberries, papaya, mango, goji, kiwi, cherries and blueberries just to name a few.

Some studies have advised that vitamin C helps to reduce fat deposition on a calorie-laden diet.

Replace yogurt and milk with avocado, doused almonds, cashew nuts, or coconut oil and add ice or water.

This substitutions will leave you with savory smoothies for weight reduction maximization.

Lastly, in my opinion smoothies should be a fast and entertaining way to load up on nutrient elements in a convenient and succulent way in order that you can meet your weight management goals.

My rule of thumb is if I can make a healthy smoothie in 5 minutes and if it tastes delicious on top of it, I keep it in my collection of smoothies for weight loss. If it is taking me more than 5 minutes and if it is too complicated to make, I do not consider the recipe because if a recipe takes too long it is in my opinion unrealistic and I will not make it again for productivity reasons.

If I like the taste of it I try to give it a chance and experiment with the ingredients by removing assorted ingredients or preparation steps until I am satisfied with the time factor. I like the formula of 5 minute quick while the recipe is still packed with maximum nutrient content.

All the recipes that are included in this book have been proven and tested and they all went through the 5 minute test. They all fit my 5 minute quick preparation formula and qualification because I know from personal experience and from interaction with people who want to lose weight with smoothies that the time factor plays a critical role in keeping a diet plan and a habit or not.

Today's life complexities and time constraints constantly challenge us to come up with new productivity and time management hacks.

Following work and social life challenges us to constantly fine-tune our consumption patterns and habits and the same thing applies to following a certain lifestyle or a diet.

This is the reason why I only included smoothies that fit the 5 minute preparation ritual because otherwise this would not qualify to be a realistic diet.

In my opinion the reason why the smoothie diet is so effective is because the following formula applies:

5 minute preparation time + deliciousness of the smoothies + combination of these nutrients is very healthy and beneficial for the body and brain + empowerment of a lifestyle with smoothies instead of a frustrating and failing diet that leads to another failing diet and so on

There are so many extreme and counter-productive diets that work against the body instead of with the intelligence of the body. These unhealthy and extreme diets just do not work because they are lacking all of the pieces (or at least one of the pieces) that are included in the smoothie diet formula above.

This smoothie diet is a very kind, stress less, delicious and enjoyable diet. It is a productive diet because not only are the smoothies 5 minute quick to make, but you do not feel hungry all the time and you can accomplish your tasks without thinking about food all the time.

These smoothies are keeping you productive because they help keep you energized throughout the day. The nutrients that are included in these smoothies are very powerful for the body and brain and they are empowering the body and brain to function in a very productive and beneficial way.

This in turn enable and empowers you to stick to a lifestyle (a lifestyle not a diet!) with smoothies and this in turn will help you keep and maintain a lean and clean body and mind which is the ultimate goal of a successful diet.

Now it is time to get started with these healthy and delicious smoothies and it is up to you to make it happen and to take responsibility for giving your body and mind clean and nutritious food.

Make sure to include these healthy Smoothies into your diet and ultimately into your lifestyle and become a clean and lean you.

You can get started today!

I have a lot of fun experimenting with these smoothie recipes for weight loss, and I hope that these healthy weight loss smoothies are getting you started with your own goal, too.

There's a lot of satisfaction when you stumble on a healthy smoothie recipe for weight loss that tastes fantastic. It's more gratifying if the recipe is 5 minute simple to make and if it is helping you shed pounds at the same time.

Don't be afraid to add or remove ingredients to make a smoothie recipe your own and as Ann Wigmore, one of the front-runners of today's raw food movement, declared, "Be creative; you just need to understand approximately what to do."

When you do make changes, jot them down! There is little worse than playing around and making a great smoothie recipe only to realise you can't remember precisely what you probably did. By making smoothies that you adore, you'll find yourself anticipating your smoothie breakfast or break snack.

Since they're so high in nourishment, you will begin to feel more fit.

If you're like me, you may also find that the more that you drink smoothies for weight loss, the more that you will begin to enjoy healthier food options like salads and fresh items. Convenience foods like potato chips will begin to taste tasteless.

The additional energy you get from the fruit, vegetable and plant based smoothies will also assist you in working out more.

All this mixed will assist in making your dieting efforts a big success!

I attempted to make this Smoothies weight management system as easy, fascinating, inspiring, easy to use and as practical to consume as possible for you because a system like this has to be compatible with today's moving and mobile world.

Just keep the book on your portable gadget next to your working table and go through one recipe at a time and as you progress with your weight reduction challenge.

The book is intended to be used in an interactive and stimulating fashion and to empower you to take action at the same time.

Remember the smoothies are 5 minute quick to prepare so this even works for the busiest person in the world.

Ultimately, the goal of this book is to lead you to a healthy lifestyle that includes healthy smoothies and food choices.

You can start with a Smoothie diet first. Once you have shed the pounds and are satisfied with your weight loss it is important to keep off the pounds.

Including these healthy smoothies into your daily meal plans and including these healthy Smoothies into your lifestyle is what you should be aiming for as your ultimate goal, too.

Once you are at the level of including healthy smoothies into your daily lifestyle and once you are successful with keeping and maintaining your weight by choosing healthy food choices like these Smoothies, you have achieved your ultimate dieting goal!

This is a goal that you will never be able to achieve with an extreme and unhealthy diet because once the diet is over you'll regain weight and you'll be starting yet another fashionable diet again. This is a plan for error and disaster and it is called the Yo-Yo effect.

The plan of the Smoothie diet, however, is very kind and intelligent because it follows the rules of the body. It nourishes and energizes the body throughout the day with all the beneficial ingredients and nutrients that are beneficial for the body and mind and it keeps your body and mind productive all the time.

I hope you will use and consume the content whenever you need some inspiration and motivation for making some healthy Smoothie recipes that are either helping you with your weight loss goal or that you just like to include into your daily meal plan because you are already living the healthy lifestyle.

Remember, all you have to do is open the book and start with the first smoothie preparation. Go through all of them and apply them on a daily basis as you see fit and depending on the health or weight loss goals that you are looking to achieve.

You will soon see for yourself that making these Smoothies is a lot of fun plus a lifestyle with Smoothies is going to make you very happy, lean and clean.

Weight Loss With Smoothies Quiz

A	I	O	A	F	M	W	C	K	C	H	I	A	U	O
V	F	G	H	C	L	K	A	L	E	P	F	E	X	F
V	L	C	W	U	X	F	G	U	D	P	P	F	M	D	Q
A	Q	V	L	T	R	E	F	P	A	P	A	Y	A	T
E	V	C	D	B	H	S	B	D	E	H	V	W	T	W
T	A	V	O	C	A	D	O	J	P	J	Q	I	J	C
D	S	G	L	U	J	S	P	I	N	A	C	H	R	W
L	L	Y	O	P	A	R	S	L	E	Y	G	H	W	Y
D	P	O	M	E	G	R	A	N	A	T	E	W	T	C
K	I	W	I	H	W	B	L	U	E	B	E	R	R	Y
B	S	R	M	W	C	K	A	H	X	R	B	E	R	B
G	I	N	G	E	R	P	A	U	K	W	R	U	W	S
K	X	R	A	T	R	Y	H	L	H	P	X	Y	M	S
S	D	W	D	B	B	E	F	N	W	Q	H	U	S	S
F	J	L	I	S	H	K	D	K	F	P	G	E	R	G

All you have to do is find 10 Smoothie Ingredient related words. Use your imagination, read backwards, sideways, and forwards to find the correct Smoothie related words and associations. Go to the next page to see the correct answers! Have fun:)

Quiz Answers

1. Kale
2. Blueberry
3. Pomegranate
4. Spinach
5. Ginger
6. Papaya
7. Parsley
8. Chia
9. Kiwi
10. Avocado

About the Publisher

InfinitYou is a hybrid general interest trade publisher. One of the first of its kind InfinitYou publishes physical books, electronic books, and audiobooks in various genres. Our publications are meant to educate, edify and entertain readers of all walks of life from babies to the elderly. Home to more than twenty imprints such as Infinit Baby, Infinit Kids, Infinit Girl, Infinit Boy, Infinit Coloring, Infinit Swear Words, Infinit Activities, Infinit Productivity, Infinit Cat, Infinit Dog, Infinit Love, Infinit Family, Infinit Survival, Infinit Health, Infinit Beauty, Infinit Spirituality, Infinit Lifestyle, Infinit Wealth, Infinit Romance, and lots more.

www.ingramcontent.com/pod-product-compliance
Lightning Source LLC
LaVergne TN
LVHW012126070526
838202LV00056B/5874